Ivor Novello's

The Dancing Years

Lyrics by
Christopher Hassall

A new version for the theatre adapted by
Cecil Clarke
and
Tom Arnold

Samuel French – London
New York – Sydney – Toronto – Hollywood

© 1939 BY CHAPPELL & CO. LTD
© 1953 BY SAMUEL FRENCH LTD
© 1985 (book revised and rewritten) BY TOM ARNOLD

ISBN 0 573 08067 4

CHARACTERS

Goetzer, an SS officer
Rudi Kleber, a composer
Grete, a young girl
Hattie, a housekeeper
Franzel, a young officer
Lilli
Elizabeth
1st Young Man
Hilde } Ladies and Gentlemen-about-town
Wanda
2nd Young Man
3rd Young Man
4th Young Man
Maria Zeigler, an operetta star
Prince Charles Metterling
Cacille Kurt, a music teacher
Ballet Mistress
Otto Breitkopf, a composer
Ceruti, a tenor
Countess Lotte
Maria's Dresser
Hans, a youth
Oscar, a head waiter
Carl, Maria's 12 year old son
A Postman, a Milkmaid, Ladies and Gentlemen-about-town, Singers and Dancers, Guests at the Gala, Footmen, Guests in Locher's restaurant, Waiters

SYNOPSIS OF SCENES

ACT I

SCENE 1* The SS headquarters in Vienna. 1938
SCENE 2 The beer garden of an inn outside Vienna. 1911
SCENE 3 A corner of the beer garden
SCENE 4 The same
SCENE 5 Maria Zeigler's drawing-room
SCENE 6 The stage of the Theater an der Wein during rehearsal. A week
           later. Transformation into a performance of *Lorelei*
SCENE 7 The corridor of the Theater an der Wein during the interval
SCENE 8 The Theater an der Wein, the second part of the performance of
           Lorelei
SCENE 9 A corridor of the Theater an der Wein. The same night
SCENE 10 A room in Maria Zeigler's apartment

ACT II

SCENE 1 The garden of a schloss outside Vienna. 1914
SCENE 2 The same
SCENE 3 A corner of the schloss garden
SCENE 4 The garden of the schloss outside Vienna
SCENE 5 A corner of the schloss garden
SCENE 6 The garden of a schloss outside Vienna
SCENE 7 A corner of the Gala setting near Vienna
SCENE 8 The Gala near Vienna
SCENE 9 Locher's restaurant, Vienna. 1927
SCENE 10 The beer garden of an inn outside Vienna. Finale

*The inclusion of Scene 1 in the SS headquarters is entirely optional. If it is
omitted the play will start with Scene 2 in the beer garden.

MUSICAL NUMBERS

The numbers in the second column under the heading v/s refer to the musical numbers in the vocal score published separately by Chappell & Co. Ltd, and available from Samuel French Ltd. The numbers in the third column under the heading c/s refer to the page numbers of the conductor's score which is only available on hire from Samuel French Ltd.

ACT I

	v/s	c/s		
(a)	—	—	**Percussion Effect**	
(b)	1	1	**Overture**	Orchestra
(c)	3	9	**Incidental Waltz**	Orchestra
(d)			**Improvised piano piece**	Piano
(e)	4	10	**Uniform**	Orchestra
(f)	5	12	**Waltz Of My Heart**	Rudi, Chorus
(g)	5	12	**Waltz Of My Heart** (Piano Reprise)	Piano
(h)	5a	13a	**Waltz Of My Heart**	Maria
(i)	5	12	**Waltz Of My Heart** (Reprise)	Chorus
(j)	6	20	**Melos**	Orchestra
(k)	7	21	**Incidental Waltz**	Orchestra
(l)	7	21	**Incidental Waltz** (Reprise)	Orchestra
(m)	9a	28	**The Wings Of Sleep** (Duet)	Maria, Cacille
(n)	11	39	**Schottische** (page 45 in v/s)	Piano
(o)	11	37	**Polka** (page 43 in v/s)	Piano
(p)	10a / 10	64 / 63	**My Life Belongs To You** (Duet)	Maria, Ceruti
(q)	11a	56	**Lady Enchanting** (O, page 144 in v/s)	Orchestra
	11a	56	**Lady Enchanting** (P and Q, pages 144 and 145 in v/s)	Lorelei, Male Chorus
(r)	11a	56	**Playout music** (P, page 144 in v/s)	Orchestra
(s)	13	67	**I Can Give You The Starlight**	Maria
(t)	13	67	**I Can Give You The Starlight**	Orchestra

ACT II

(aa)	p.153	95	**When It's Spring In Vienna**	Cacille, Chorus
(bb)	15	70b	**My Dearest Dear**	Maria
(cc)	16	72	**Chorale and Tyrolese Dance**	Chorus
(dd)			**Music**	Orchestra
(ee)	18	80	**Primrose**	Grete
(ff)	18a	85	**My Dearest Dear** (Reprise)	Piano
(gg)	18a	85	**My Dearest Dear** (Reprise)	Piano
(hh)	21	98	**The Leap Year Waltz**	Orchestra
(ii)	23	111	**Incidental Music**	Orchestra
(jj)	24	112	**Waltz**	Orchestra
(kk)	26	116	**Incidental Waltz**	Orchestra
(ll)	5a	13a	**Waltz Of My Heart**	Orchestra
(mm)	26a	117	**My Dearest Dear** (Reprise)	Orchestra
(nn)	13	66	**I Can Give You The Starlight**	Orchestra
(oo)	26a	117	**My Dearest Dear** (Reprise)	Maria
(pp)	28	120	**Finale**	Company

THE DANCING YEARS

The Dancing Years was first produced at the Theatre Royal, Drury Lane, in March, 1939. Its run was terminated on 31st August—three days before the declaration of war. A year later it began an eighteen-month tour, and it returned to the Adelphi Theatre in March, 1942, where it ran for 969 performances. With a further tour and another London season it played almost continuously for a decade. Since then it has been produced by many hundreds of amateur societies, although its heavy scene plot, the resources required (it included a "Masque of Vienna" in two parts, and an excerpt from *Lorelei*—an opera within the play), and a running time of nearly three and a half hours have restricted it to groups with very considerable resources.

Recently, Cecil Clarke did an adaptation for television, and this has been used as the basis for the current version. While retaining all the well-known musical numbers, it allows a more fluid production, no longer dependent upon major scene changes, and, by omitting scenes incidental to the main plot, has concentrated on the central love story.

The closing scene of the original, in which Ivor Novello intended to give the play special topicality by contrasting the happiness of the "dancing years" with Nazi tyranny, is now included as an optional preface.

TEXTUAL NOTE

As staging for this adapted version has been greatly simplified and the sets left very much to the individual director and the resources available, no furniture and property list has been included in this Acting Edition.

A black line in the foredge margin indicates where music from the separately published vocal score is used. The numbers which head the black lines refer to the musical numbers of the vocal score unless a specific reference is made to the page number.

ACT I*

Scene 1

Goetzer's office at the SS headquarters in Vienna. 1938. Day. (N.B. This scene is entirely optional and may be omitted in which case Act I begins with Scene 2 in the beer garden)

When the Curtain *rises the stage is in darkness*

(a) Music

There is the sound track of a goose-stepping march. Orchestral percussion only underneath (this is not in the vocal score and should be devised by the director, musical director and sound effects supervisor)

Suddenly, dim lighting comes up on two Nazi soldiers upstage and huge Nazi flags appear and threateningly flutter in the breeze. The orchestral percussion and sound effect reach a climax and suddenly stop

Immediately, two white, harsh spots come up on SS Captain Goetzer R *and Rudi Kleber, who is in his fifties,* L

Goetzer Herr Kleber, you have helped a great number of people to escape——
Rudi —people who only wished to leave a country which clearly has no further use for them.
Goetzer Allow me to continue. My superiors are most concerned at the way in which you have abused your position, bribed our officials and made a mockery of the administration. We are prepared to release you and, provided you stop these subversive activities, we shall remove the ban on both you and your music.
Rudi That is most generous of you. What you really mean is my music is too popular and too national in spirit to be suppressed. And your superiors— if there are any grades of superiority in your organization——
Goetzer Being cynical will not help you.
Rudi Cynical? I intended to be insulting. You can tell those "superiors" of yours that as long as I live I shall do just what I'm doing now. Do you think this ban on my music here in our country has killed it for the world outside? You can't touch it. It's there—to remind everyone there was once a place called Vienna where the only crime was to be happy.
Goetzer Be careful, Herr Kleber. You have a simple choice, but be warned: if you are arrested again, you won't be released.

The spot on Goetzer snaps off

Goetzer exits R

---

*N.B. Paragraph 3 on page ii of this Acting Edition regarding photocopying and video-recording should be carefully read.

The Lights upstage fade to Black-out and the flags are taken out

The two Nazi Soldiers exit

Rudi turns to his left and starts to exit with the spot following him

Maria Zeigler, also in her fifties, enters L and a spot comes up on her. The spots on both Rudi and Maria now have some warmth in the colour

Maria Rudi, are you all right? I came as soon as I heard they were letting you go. What have they done to you?

Rudi Nothing . . . yet. They just threatened me to try and stop me helping people to escape.

Maria The bullies are getting stronger every day—turning our whole world upside down.

Rudi All the more reason for me to carry on resisting them. I don't mind the danger. Even when they locked me up, I didn't mind—my thoughts were far away, somewhere with you—back over the years. The Dancing Years—some happy, some sad, but all so full of wonderful memories.

Maria For both of us. They'll come again. And you know what they will say. You made the whole world dance.

Maria and Rudi turn to look upstage

No. 1   **(b) Overture**

The orchestra plays a selection of tunes arranged from the "Overture" to the required length for Grete's entrance

A small figure, Grete, appears in a spot upstage C. She is fifteen, with blond hair in plaits. She is barefooted

Rudi and Maria exit

Grete starts to move downstage, dancing in a carefree, happy way. The music is a mixture of the main themes. As she reaches halfway, the beer garden set for Scene 2 begins to form. Grete finishes her dance at the right musical moment and starts to get water from the pump

A Postman crosses the stage

Grete and the Postman greet each other sleepily. The music continues until Rudi's entrance

Rudi enters. He is now about thirty, dark and good-looking

SCENE 2

The beer garden of an inn outside Vienna. 1911. Dawn—5 a.m.

The Lights come up to give a dawn effect on the beer garden of a small inn which has a few rooms where people can stay, although we do not actually see the inn building. There are a few tables about with chairs and small benches stacked on them. There is a small grand piano covered with a cloth. On top of it is a basket full of music manuscripts and a piano stool. There is a small water pump in one corner

During the following, Rudi washes his face in pump water and uses Grete's apron to wipe his face

Grete Rudi, why are you up so early?

Rudi I couldn't sleep, worrying about my piano out here all night. It might have rained. I still can't understand why your Aunt Liesel moved it out.

Grete I told you. It's now Summer. People sit out here, so that's where you must play.

Rudi I can't do it. They are all so noisy and they never listen. Anyway, my music is written to be played in the theatre, not in a vulgar beer garden.

Grete Rudi, you have no choice. You need the money the customers give you to pay your rent. So why not accept it! Aunt Liesel is getting fed up with you. You sit in your room writing music and dreaming, when you should be working.

Rudi Why shouldn't I dream? I dream of conducting my own operetta at the Theater an der Wien. (*He sits at the piano*) For heaven's sake, I must have something to aim for.

Grete Rudi, I understand. It's a lovely dream and I know it will come true.

Rudi starts to play an improvisation of the "Incidental Waltz"

You can't play now. You'll wake everyone.

Rudi plays a few bars and then stops

Is it all right?

Rudi Yes, it seems to like being out all night.

The Postman appears having delivered mail. He is amused by Rudi playing the piano at such an early hour. He exits

Incidental Waltz   No. 3

Rudi plays the waltz. The Orchestra join in and Rudi and Grete dance

Hattie enters. She is a warm, comfortable person who is cook and housekeeper

Rudi and Grete stop dancing

Rudi Hattie! You gave me a fright. I thought for a moment you were Aunt Liesel.

Hattie Are you both mad—dancing around at five o'clock in the morning. You'll wake her up.

Rudi After what she's done, I couldn't care. My piano will be ruined out here.

Hattie You can't stay here for six months for nothing. Anywhere else you would have been thrown out long ago. Now, help me get this place ready. I've people coming in half an hour for breakfast.

Rudi We'll help—if you give us some breakfast.

Hattie You'll get breakfast after I've served all the others. Grete, go and get the knives and forks and take that water in.

Grete goes off with the bucket

Rudi (*helping Hattie with the tables etc.*) Who's coming?

Hattie Some young men and their actress friends. They spend all night drinking and then come here for breakfast to sober up. I suppose you know that Aunt Liesel is threatening to turn you out?

Rudi Again?

Hattie This time she means it and, what's more, she's going to sell your piano.

Rudi She's what? Why?

Hattie To cover the rent you owe.

Rudi How much is she asking for it?

Hattie Five hundred kronen and Schollmeyer's coming at nine to look at it.

Rudi It's worth more than that! How much do I owe?

Hattie Five hundred kronen.

Rudi I'll get it before nine.

Hattie You'll have to look slippy.

Hattie exits

(d) Music

Rudi goes to the piano, sits and plays a sad little piece. This should be an improvisation based on any number in the score, but it must be sad. Rudi continues playing throughout the following

Grete enters with a box of knives and forks which she puts on a table

Grete Rudi, what's the matter? You look sad.

Rudi Your aunt wants to sell my piano and Schollmeyer's coming at nine.

Grete Oh Rudi, I'm so sorry. What can we do?

Rudi I don't know. Oh, Grete, I sometimes wonder whether anyone but you will ever listen to my music.

Grete One day the whole world will listen and you will be very famous and forget all about me. I wish I could grow up quickly.

Rudi Don't you like being fifteen?

Grete No, and by the time I'm ready for you, you will probably be past it.

Rudi Oh, thank you. (*He stops playing*)

Grete And now, come on in. I've taken some bread and cheese up to your room. We can have breakfast before the crowd arrive.

Rudi Grete, you're an angel and I love you.

Grete Because I got breakfast?

Rudi Other reasons too.

Grete Come on, quickly!

Rudi and Grete exit

The Lights fade quickly to Black-out. Then a strobe lighting effect accom-

panies the following music to give the impression of a time lapse with people arriving. The whole effect should be carefully choreographed

(e) Uniform (music)

No. 4

An arrangement of "Uniform" can be used without the vocal

> *Men and women enter throughout the strobe effect. The men are a mixture of Officers and Young Men about town. The ladies are Young Actresses and Dancers including Lilli, Hilde, Wanda and Elizabeth*

When the arrival of the men and women is complete the Lights change to give a bright morning sunshine effect

At the end of the number they disperse, some sit, some explore

> *Franzel enters. He is a young officer*

Lilli Franzel, where have you been?
Franzel Paying off the cabs.
Elizabeth What about breakfast? Franzel, you said there would be breakfast.
Franzel So there will be. I spoke to Hattie myself.
Lilli And who might Hattie be?
Franzel The best cook in the world. I'll go and find her.
1st Man If she's still in bed we'll go and pull her out.

Franzel and some men move to exit

> *Hattie enters. Grete follows Hattie and starts to lay knives and forks on table*

Hattie Oh, you will, will you? Bigger boys than you have tried to pull me out of bed, and into it ...
1st Man And did they succeed, Hattie?
Hattie That's neither here nor there. Now sit down or you won't get your bacon and eggs.

> *Hattie exits*

Hilde Bacon and eggs—how lovely!
Wanda I adore English food. What a pity Maria didn't come. Breakfast here was her idea.
2nd Man Will there be music with breakfast?
Grete Why not? I know the best pianist in the world, but he's very expensive.
Franzel How expensive?
Grete He'd want at least twenty kronen.
Franzel I think we can manage that.
Grete He may want more. I'll go and ask him.

> *Grete exits*

Lilli Pretty girl.
3rd Man Franzel!

Franzel Good lord, a grand piano—business must be looking up. (*He goes over and sits at the piano, striking some notes*)

Rudi enters

Rudi Will you please leave my piano alone.
Franzel *Your* piano?
Rudi Certainly.
Lilli So you're the "best pianist in the world"?
Rudi And a composer.
Franzel What do you compose? Symphonies, operas?
Rudi No, just waltzes.
Franzel Just waltzes—what a relief! Perhaps we might hear one whilst we have breakfast.
Rudi Certainly, but I only play for money.
Franzel How much?
Rudi Thirty kronen.
Lilli The young girl said twenty!
Rudi No—thirty.
Franzel (*to Lilli*) You're quite mistaken, she said thirty. Thank you, Herr——
Rudi Kleber. Rudi Kleber. And what is your name?
Franzel Franzel von Wilmetz.

Rudi shakes his hand

Rudi I will play you my latest waltz. Here are some copies of it. You can follow it if you wish. (*He strikes a note on piano several times*) Don't let me interrupt the conversation. Anyway, I'll only be playing for myself.
4th Man Quiet everybody. He wants to start.
Franzel There's no extra change for listening?
Rudi I hadn't thought of that.
Elizabeth (*reading the manuscript*) "Waltz Of My Heart".

No. 5   **(f) Waltz Of My Heart**

Rudi (*playing and singing*)
> The lark is singing on high
> The sun's ashine in the blue,
> The winter is driven away
> And spring is returning anew.

Chorus join in la-ing as Rudi continues

All
> Who cares what sorrow may bring
> What storms may tear us apart?
> No sadness can kill
> The wonder and thrill
> Of that waltz in my heart.

Franzel You were right to ask for thirty kronen. It's a charming tune.
Rudi Would you like to buy it?
Franzel Is it for sale?
Rudi They're all for sale. I've several more. I have a few debts to pay and it would help if you bought it. Who knows, I might be famous one day.

All of the next exchanges must be very quick to build up the sense of bidding at an auction

Lilli I would like a waltz of my own!

Wanda Me too!

1st Man Steady on—he'll rob us!

Rudi No, just give me what you think it's worth.

1st Man What about fifty kronen?

Franzel I'd go to seventy-five.

2nd Man Eighty.

3rd Man Ninety.

Franzel One hundred kronen and that's it.

4th Man A hundred and ten!

Lilli Oh!

2nd Man A hundred and twenty-five.

Hilde (*to 1st Man*) Oh please, I really would love a waltz of my own!

1st Man Very well—one hundred and fifty!

Rudi A hundred and fifty. I'll play it again and perhaps you will offer more.

1st Man I think a hundred and fifty's enough.

(g) Waltz Of My Heart (Piano Reprise)   No. 5

Rudi plays the refrain again and the Guests waltz

   Maria Zeigler approaches. She is an attractive woman of about thirty. Grete returns

Maria I'll give you five hundred for that waltz.

Rudi stops playing

   Five hundred kronen. Well, are you all struck dumb? Isn't anyone going to outbid me?

Hilde Maria, we'd given you up.

1st Man Just in time for breakfast.

Maria (*to Rudi*) Well, what do you say?

Rudi If you offer five hundred kronen, it must be a *very* good waltz.

Maria I don't know about that—but it happens to be just what I'm looking for in my new operetta.

Rudi Who's written the music?

Maria Otto Brietkopf.

Rudi You have my deepest sympathy.

Maria Oh! What is your name?

Rudi Rudi Kleber.

Maria I'm Maria Zeigler.

Rudi Maria Zeigler.

Maria No doubt you've seen me?

Rudi No, I can't afford theatre tickets.

Maria But you know who I am?

Rudi Yes. Everyone in Vienna knows who you are. And now, may I please have my five hundred kronen? If I don't have the money by nine o'clock, they'll take away my piano.

Maria Why?

Rudi I owe my landlady here six months' rent and she's beginning to lose confidence.

Maria Tell her I will be responsible.

Rudi No. That wouldn't be right. I will pay for it with my waltz.

Maria You mean with my money?

Rudi It's the same thing.

Maria Franzel, have you got five hundred kronen?

Franzel Not on me.

Maria Then we must make a collection.

Maria goes round the crowd with Franzel's hat collecting money. Grete gets under the piano

Maria Here, Herr Kleber, is your money.

Rudi And here is your waltz.

Maria No, *your* waltz. That five hundred only gives me the exclusive right to sing it—then it will be published and you will make more money. Why are you looking so worried?

Rudi I must get a message to Schollmeyer by nine o'clock. Where's Grete?

Grete crawls from under the piano

Grete! There you are! (*To Maria*) This is my friend, Grete Schone. (*To Grete*) That's Maria Zeigler. Run to Schollmeyer and tell him Aunt Liesel is not now going to sell my piano. I can pay her the rent I owe now.

Grete But Maria Zeigler gave you the money.

Rudi Nobody *gave* me the money. I earned it with my music.

Grete Oh Rudi—your dream!

Grete exits. As she goes, she acknowledges the Milkmaid who enters with milk buckets and exits to other side of the stage

Elizabeth What a charming girl.

Maria Is she a relation?

Rudi No, just a friend. She wants to marry me—she will, too, if I'm not careful.

2nd Man Ah, breakfast!

Hattie and a Youth, Hans, appear with large trays of breakfast things

Franzel Maria—breakfast.

They all sit

Maria Herr Kleber—won't you join us?

Rudi No, thank you—the sight of all that money has taken my appetite away. I will play for you while you eat.

Rudi plays a showy improvisation on the piano and when he suddenly stops, Maria speaks

Maria Please, go on.

Rudi Not unless you sing for us.

Maria No. It's too early in the morning.
Rudi Oh please.

The Milkmaid appears without the buckets and three passers-by, two women and a man enter

Hattie and Hans join the listeners. Maria rises and sings

(h) Waltz Of My Heart   No. 5a

Maria   Waltz of my heart
           Haunting and gay,
           Calling enthrallingly
           Waltzing away.
           Ring out your bells for me,
           Ivory keys,
           Weave out your spells for me
           Orchestra, please!
           Chorus of wings
           Thrilling the sky,
           While you're inspiring me
           Time hurries by,
           Joy fans a fire in me
           Soon as you start
           Sweeping your strings,
           Waltz of my heart.
           The lark is singing on high
           The sun's ashine in the blue,
           The winter is driven away
           And spring is returning anew.
           Who cares what sorrow may bring,
           What storms may tear us apart.
           No sadness can kill
           The wonder and thrill
           Of that waltz in my heart.

The Lights fade (leaving perhaps the sky effect) to spots on Maria and Rudi and a solo violin plays. There is a Black-out at the end of the solo

   Rudi and Maria exit

The moment of darkness is covered by music which becomes the introduction to the next number

(i) Waltz Of My heart (Reprise)   No. 5

The Lights come up to full and the Chorus reprise "The lark is singing on high". Choreograph the number and their exit

   During the number, Hattie and Hans clear the breakfast remains, and at the end of the number the Chorus exit

Immediately, a light piece of scenery (not a cloth) is dropped in downstage to

*hide the beer garden. It should represent another part of the garden. During the
next scene, Maria's room is set behind this front piece*

No. 6   **(j) Melos**

> *Hans enters and sets a bench downstage*
>
> *The music to cover the scene change can go on during Maria and Charles's
> entrance. The Lights change to give a daylight effect*

Scene 3

A corner of the beer garden. Morning

*Hans has just finished setting the bench and starts to exit. Charles and
Maria enter, ad libbing as they come on*

Charles (*calling to Hans*) Coffee, please, here. (*To Maria*) I suppose they
have coffee in this beer-drinking place.

Hans exits

Maria Charles, you're being difficult.

Charles I'm not being difficult, but I would like to know exactly why you
have brought me here.

Maria I've told you. I've found a genius, and I want you to use your
influence with the directors of the Theater an der Wien—this man has
talent.

Charles Yes, and looks.

Maria I hadn't noticed.

Charles Maria—what are you up to?

Maria A great deal.

Charles Oh, you can tell me—I shan't be hurt—I gave up being that a long
time ago.

Maria When?

Charles The first time I found you out.

Maria With the Italian! I was livid with you. I said I'd marry you, but you
looked straight through me. An unknown chorus girl couldn't possibly
marry into the noble house of Metterling! But now I'm a success, it would
be just the thing!

*Hans enters with two cups of coffee, cream and sugar on a tray. He puts the
tray on the bench and exits*

Charles (*suddenly, after Hans has gone*) Maria—will you marry me? Now—
today?

Maria Are you serious? (*She takes her coffee from the tray*)

Charles Yes.

Maria Coffee?

Charles shakes his head

You ordered it. But why so suddenly? You've never asked me before.

Charles Because I have a strong feeling I'm going to lose you—I mean it, Maria, will you?

Maria No, Charles—we know too much about each other. When I marry . . .

Rudi enters

Rudi Fräulein Zeigler, I've packed all my things—where shall I tell them to send my piano?

Maria Palais Metterling—Weberstrasse Ten. (*She puts down her coffee cup*)

Charles Maria——

Maria Isn't it generous of Prince Metterling. A studio at the top of his house—ideal. (*To Charles*) It's charming of you. Thank you, Charles. (*To Rudi*) Herr Kleber, why don't you go and put your things into the carriage.

Rudi Yes.

Rudi goes

Charles Really, Maria. I can stand most things, but that man staying in my house——

Maria You won't see much of him. I'll soon take him off your hands.

Maria exits

(k) Incidental Waltz

No. 7

Charles You know, Maria, you can be very aggravating sometimes and it makes me uneasy.

Charles follows Maria

The music can quietly carry over into the next scene and stop at the director's discretion

SCENE 4

The same. Day

Grete enters with a pair of Rudi's boots

Grete Rudi, you forgot to pack your boots! (*She suddenly realizes that he is not there. She pauses. Calling*) Rudi! Rudi! Rudi! (*She looks around, drops the boots and gradually becomes panic-stricken. Shouting loudly*) Rudi—Rudi!

Hattie enters

Hattie Whatever's the matter?

Grete Oh Hattie—he's gone and he didn't even say goodbye.

Hattie He wouldn't leave you like that.

Rudi enters

(*Seeing Rudi*) Come on, dry your eyes. (*She gives Grete a handkerchief*)

Hattie picks up the coffee tray and goes

Rudi Grete ...

Grete Oh, Rudi—you've come back—you didn't forget.

Rudi Forget?

Grete I thought I wasn't going to see you again. You're all I've got—you will wait for me, won't you?

Rudi My dear child, don't you realize you're all I've got?

Grete Child—there you are, you see—that's all I am to you—but I won't always be. Promise ...

Rudi What?

Grete Promise you'll never ask her or anyone to marry you until you've seen if I'm good enough.

Rudi Good enough?

Grete I may grow up awful—and if I do you just say—"You're awful now, you used not to be"—but give me a chance. No, don't laugh. I really mean this—promise.

Rudi smiles

Not with a smile. Look at me and say it.

Rudi Grete Schone, I promise never to ask anyone to marry me ...

Grete Until I've given you—go on.

Rudi Until I've given you ...

Grete The first refusal.

Rudi The first refusal.

Grete And you'll never tell a soul in the world?

Rudi Not if you don't want me to, no.

Grete I don't. Now I feel safe.

Rudi I must go now.

Grete Yes.

Rudi I'll be back.

Grete When?

Rudi Soon.

Grete Go on—you mustn't keep them waiting.

Rudi They kept me waiting for years.

> *Rudi goes*

No. 7   **(1) Incidental Waltz** (Reprise)

Grete follows him to wave goodbye. The Lights fade to a spot on Grete who moves downstage. She is fighting to keep back her tears and as she goes, she sees the boots where she dropped them. She picks them up, holding them close to her

> *Grete exits*

The front piece is flown out

> *Hans enters and takes the bench off*

Anticipate the vocal exercises which open Scene 5 so that we hear them before we see Cacille Kurt and Maria

SCENE 5

Maria's drawing-room. One month later. Day

The Lights come up on Frau Cacille Kurt and Maria practising scales. Kurt is sitting at the piano. Maria sings one scale, then sings another

Kurt Now, a little brighter tone. (*She does a scale to demonstrate*)

Maria does the same and then stops in a more or less temperamental manner

Maria Oh, I can't—I'm tired—all those rehearsals.

Kurt Your voice isn't tired at all. Maria, you've no discipline. When I had to sing a new part I went to bed for a week.

Maria Who with?

Kurt That's beside the point—Maria, you're very wicked!

Maria Well, so were you—when you were my age.

Kurt Come on. Who is it?

Maria No-one.

Kurt Don't lie to me—who is it?

Maria It's ridiculous. A composer.

Kurt A composer? Fatal!

Maria That's just what it is—fatal! I put him in a lovely studio and he totally ignores me! How dare he be late!

Kurt Maria, in all the years you have studied with me I have never known you like this! You must pull yourself together.

Maria How can I sing his music if he hates me? No, he doesn't hate me, he doesn't even know I'm here. You must believe me, for the first time, I am in love.

Kurt laughs

No, don't laugh. It's true. For the first time I want to marry—to have a home—children—I would even give up the stage——

A door bangs shut

That must be him!

Charles enters

It's you, Charles.

Charles Obviously.

Maria Well, you can't stay, we're in the middle of our lesson.

Charles Your lesson? Of course. Frau Kurt, forgive me for interrupting.

Kurt You're not interrupting. Maria's impossible. I can't get her to sing a note.

Maria I'm all on edge.

Charles You should relax, get away from it all. I was going to suggest supper tonight.

Maria No, not tonight.

Charles Tomorrow?

Maria No, I've promised Breitkopf.

Charles Breitkopf. Are you still speaking to him since you threw out his last song?

Maria That man wrote his last song twenty years ago. He's a has-been.

Charles Never mind, we've several young up and coming composers.

Maria Who?

Charles Well, there's Rudolf Kleber—and Rudi Kleber—and Rudi and Kleber ...

Maria Charles, sarcasm doesn't suit you.

Charles Sarcasm! Not at all—only I was wondering what had happened to the days when you were free for supper every evening—rehearsals or no.

Maria That was before I took my work seriously.

Charles Or before you took yourself seriously?

Maria Charles, do go now, you're interrupting our work.

Charles Ah, work and more work.

Rudi suddenly enters

Rudi Hello, Charles.

Maria At last? You are late.

Rudi I'm sorry.

Maria Rudi, this is my beloved teacher Frau Kurt.

Rudi goes to Kurt and bends as he kisses her hand

(*To Charles*) And now, Charles, please go—we really must work.

Charles I had hoped you would allow me to stay.

Maria No.

Charles Very well. Goodbye, and don't work too hard—emotionally.

Charles exits

Rudi You must forgive me. I'm feeling sad today. (*To Kurt*) My young friend, Grete, has gone away to school in England.

Kurt Poor child.

Rudi She'll be all right. She was unhappy for a time after her aunt died, but not now.

Maria You'll miss her, I'm sure.

Kurt And now, if you two have finished, I have been here for over an hour ...

Maria I'm sorry. Rudi, you do realize that this is Frau *Cacille* Kurt?

Rudi Frau Cacille Kurt! Do you know my father once walked all the way from Innsbruk to hear you sing Isolde?

Kurt Ah, I was a soprano then, but later, I became a contralto. It's not much fun singing contralto. In a few years, I shall be basso profundo. (*She sings a scale, going down to a very low register*)

Rudi Good heavens, what a wind.

Kurt Well, now—let's do some work.

Maria What shall we do first—the duet, "The Wings of Sleep". Cacille, sing it with me. (*She gives Kurt a copy of the manuscript*)

Kurt (*to Rudi*) Is it one of yours?

Rudi Yes.

Maria Rudi played it for us so much at rehearsal, that in desperation we put it in.

Rudi Nonsense—you put it in because it was better than the song you had.

Rudi starts to play

(m) Wings Of Sleep   No. 9a

Maria }	Soon as the shades are falling
Kurt }	Gently calling you to rest;
	All the bright hours forgetting,
	Slowly setting in the west,
Kurt	Music begins to fill the sky
	With a slow lullaby,
Both	Soothing and softly smoothing cares away
	From the noisy day.
Maria	When night is dark and deep
	And shepherds count their sheep,
Kurt	You'll hear in the silver silence
	The whispering wings of sleep.
Both	They fly around your bed
	And soothe your weary head;
	So dream till dawn,
	Securely borne
	On the wings of sleep,
	The wings of sleep,
	The wings of sleep.

At the end of "Wings of Sleep" the Lights fade to Black-out

The drawing-room set and furniture are struck and an upright rehearsal piano is set downstage for Scene 6. This scene change could be done as though everything was being struck at a rehearsal, possibly in a working light atmosphere

People start coming on the stage for rehearsals of Lorelei. *These include a rehearsal pianist, Dancers and a Ballet Mistress, and a large gentleman called Otto Breitkopf, a famous composer of operetta*

(n) Schottische   No. 11

Downstage, the Dancers start an amusing "daily class" under the watchful and sharp eye of the Ballet Mistress. The Dancers limber up to the music of "Schottische" (on page 45 of the vocal score). They are watched by Otto Breitkopf. At the end of the class there is the piano introduction to "The Polka" (on page 43 of the vocal score) with all the Dancers and the Ballet Mistress

(o) "The Polka"

After the piano introduction the orchestra joins in

SCENE 6

The bare stage of the Theater an der Wein. A week later. Day

"The Polka" finishes

Ballet Mistress Disaster! Practise, practise, practise!

Maria comes in with Ceruti, a tenor. They are both wearing cloaks which hide their "performance" costumes for the transformation cover in the scene

Maria (*calling as she goes to the piano*) Rudi! I want to rehearse the love duet at the end of Act One.

No response

Where is he?

Rudi is not there, but Otto comes towards Maria

Otto Maria, there is no love duet at the end of Act One. We finish on the full chorus number, as in the score.
Maria I've changed that.
Otto Since when?
Maria Since Rudi Kleber played his new duet to me last night.

Rudi enters during the following. He carries a music manuscript

Otto But this changes everything. None of my music will be left.
Maria Exactly, Herr Otto Brietkopf. And if you listen to this, you will understand why. Where is Rudi? (*She sees Rudi*) Oh, there you are. I want to rehearse with Ceruti "My Life Belongs To You". Can we have the parts, please?
Rudi Maria, it's still in a very rough state. I've got to work on it.
Maria I want Ceruti to hear it. We'll go through it now and then you can work on it later. Give the music to the pianist.
Rudi Very well. (*He goes and gives the music to the rehearsal pianist*)

No. 10a   **(p) My Life Belongs To You** (Reprise)

Maria }
Ceruti }
My life belongs to you,
My dreams, my songs, all that I do.
No moon, no morning star can shine,
No happiness is mine
Without you near me.

Rudi disappears to the orchestra pit

When years have passed into the shade,
You'll hear my last serenade
For ever echoing anew;
No matter where you go
Your listening heart will know
My life belongs to you.

During the following, the scene transforms to the stage set for the first night performance of Lorelei—*the upright rehearsal piano is struck and a box is set on one side for Charles and another box on the opposite side for Lotte, Kurt and Franzel. When the transformation moment comes, Maria and Ceruti are* c *and the Lights fade to two spots on them giving an exterior moonlight effect*

At the same moment, Dressers, in total black (including hoods), enter and whip off Maria and Ceruti's cloaks to reveal their "performance" costumes. With the exception of Maria and Ceruti, everyone exits. Then Charles, Lotte, Kurt and Franzel enter their respective boxes and Rudi appears in the orchestra pit

My Life Belongs To You

Ceruti   When first we met
             I heard a voice within
             "The scene is set,
             And here's your heroine"
             I raised my eyes,
             My breath was taken by that sweet surprise,
             Your hand was mine
             By law divine.

The transformation is now complete; Rudi is in the orchestra pit conducting and Charles, Lotte, Kurt and Franzel in their boxes

Maria ⎫   My life belongs to you,
Ceruti ⎭   My dreams, my songs, all that I do.
             No moon, no morning star can shine,
             No happiness is mine
             Without you near me.
             When years have passed into the shade,
             You'll hear my last serenade
             For ever echoing anew;
             No matter where you go
             Your listening heart will know
             My life belongs to you.

Black-out. The corridor piece is dropped in downstage

SCENE 7

The corridor of the Theater an der Wein. That night

It is the interval during the first-night performance of Lorelei. *Small groups of people are milling about, talking. These include Franzel and Lotte who form one group and Charles who is with another group*

Franzel (*to Lotte*) Don't you think it's marvellous?
Lotte Yes, enchanting.
Franzel What about Maria?
Lotte Superb, as usual.
Franzel I keep humming that tune. (*He hums a few bars of "My Life Belongs To You"*)
Lotte Yes, we've all heard it. I simply can't wait to tell you. Can you keep a secret?

Franzel tries to answer, but Lotte carries on

Well, promise you won't tell a soul. You know how I hate gossip. I've
heard it's all off between Maria and Charles, and what's more——

Franzel (*interrupting*) It can't be.

Lotte (*ignoring Franzel's remark*) They're never seen together—they used to
ride every morning—lunch at the Coblenz, have tea together, then supper
at Locher's and now not a sight of them.

Franzel I expect Maria's been busy rehearsing.

Lotte Yes, and that's my other piece of news—what's the composer's
name—Rudi something or other.

Franzel Kleber.

Lotte They say he's the reason.

Franzel Rudi? Oh, I'm sure it's impossible. I was there when they met at six
in the morning—he played the piano.

Lotte That doesn't make him unattractive!

Franzel I'm quite sure you're wrong.

Lotte Charles told a friend of mine——

Charles comes over to Lotte

Charles Yes, Lotte, and what did Charles tell?

Lotte Hullo, Charles.

Charles You're looking charming, Lotte.

Franzel Charles, do back me up—didn't I discover our newest composer?

Charles Oh, but he did—along with several other drunken rowdies at six
o'clock in the morning.

Franzel He played the piano and Maria ...

Charles Yes, Franzel—Maria, you were going to say?

Franzel Maria turned up and bought a waltz of his.

Lotte So that's when he fell in love with her.

Charles Did he? How interesting—Maria never told me that.

Lotte It's only hearsay.

Charles Yes. I'll check with Maria tonight.

Lotte Then you *are* seeing her tonight?

Charles Of course. Maria always has supper with me after every first night.

Lotte But I thought——

Charles Oh, I shouldn't if I were you, Lotte—you're much too pretty for
that.

Lotte Really, Charles! But I'm so relieved you're seeing each other. I'm
fond of you both. I wouldn't like anything to go wrong.

Charles Well, if it does, Lotte, I'm sure you'll be the first to know!

Lotte (*reproving*) Now, Charles. I shall retire to my box and keep my opera
glasses glued to the conductor!

*A footman moves through the crowd ringing a small handbell to indicate the
end of the interval and people begin to drift off*

Come along, Franzel!

Lotte goes

Charles Franzel.

Franzel Yes?

Charles If you hear any more rumours about Maria and Kleber, you might deny them, will you?

Franzel Of course. (*He turns to go*)

Charles And, Franzel, there's something else. I have to go to London at dawn tomorrow. You might keep an eye on our protegé.

Franzel On Rudi?

Charles Yes, he's new to Vienna and very vulnerable. He doesn't yet know his way round; he might get hurt. I shouldn't like that to happen.

Franzel Of course. I'll do what I can to help him.

Charles Thank you, Franzel.

Franzel goes. Maria's Dresser comes to Charles

Dresser Your Highness—Fräulein Zeigler says, would you excuse her tonight—she's very tired and she's sure you'd understand.

Charles Understand? Did she say anything else?

Dresser She was just going on stage, but I think she said to say she was "sorry".

Charles Thank you.

No. 11a

O

The music for an excerpt from Lorelei *begins. (This will be found on page 144 of the vocal score under the heading O in the Supplementary Numbers section)*

The Dresser exits

Sorry!

Charles exits

The corridor piece is flown out and the Lights change

SCENE 8

The Theater an der Wein. The same night

The second part of the first-night performance of Lorelei. *The "stage" area has a "theatrical" set which the lighting should complement. On either side, opposite to one another, are the two theatre boxes as set previously during Scene 6*

Lotte, Kurt and Franzel are in their box, Rudi is conducting in the orchestra pit and Maria, as Lorelei, and the Male Chorus are "on stage" singing an excerpt from Lorelei *(see page 144 following of the vocal score under the headings P and Q in the Supplementary Numbers section)*

During the following, Charles enters his box, looks at Maria and Rudi, then leaves

No. 11a
P

Men	Lady entrancing, Are you not dancing? Give us an answer pray. Lady beguiling, Why are you smiling? Tell us without delay.
Lorelei	Gentlemen, gentlemen, gently I pray; Kindness like this is alarming. How can I possibly choose from you all One who is specially charming
Men	Tell us you find us quite charming.

No. 11a
Q

Lorelei	I'm a girl who always likes to say what's on my mind. Life has taught me always to be frank but not unkind. So if any man should say please to me, If I should give him leave to squeeze me, But, of you all I can find not one.

Men	She' a girl who
	  always likes to say
	
	what's on her mind.
	Life has taught her
	  always to be frank
	  but not unkind.
	So if any man should
	  please her
	
	She should give him
	  leave to squeeze her,
	But of us all
	She can find not one.
		Lorelei	Though I find you quite
			  charming,
			You really are alarming
			With your kindness
			  disarming
			
			I must make up my mind
			They're not really un-
			  kind,
			I'll do my best to choose,
			
			But now of you all
			I can find not one.

All the Dancers enter

They join with Maria in a choreographed dance routine with Maria and the Male Chorus finally going into a Reprise of the last section of the number bringing it to a grand musical climax. The Female Chorus could join in the Reprise

There is a Black-out at the end of the Reprise and the corridor piece is dropped in downstage

Rudi exits from the orchestra pit

SCENE 9

A corridor of the Theater an der Wein. The same night

(r) Playout Music

Playout music is heard faintly under this scene (this is an instrumental reprise of "Lady Enchanting" no. 11a under the heading P on page 144 of the vocal score

Some of the audience are going home. There is improvised dialogue as they exit

Lotte and Franzel enter. Franzel carries Lotte's cloak

Franzel It was a triumph. Maria must be thrilled.

They stop. Franzel helps Lotte with her cloak

Lotte I'm sure, but did you see Charles leave early? I wonder why?
Franzel Some official matter, perhaps.
Lotte On Maria's first night? Unheard of! Stop fiddling with my cloak! (*She continues towards the exit*) We must get to Locher's. Charles will be there. I'm dying to find out.

They exit

The music finishes

The corridor piece is flown out and the Lights change

SCENE 10

A room in Maria Zeigler's apartment. Later that night

Rudi Maria?
Maria (*off*) Yes?
Rudi Your champagne's getting flat.
Maria (*off*) I like it flat.
Rudi Maria?
Maria (*off*) Yes?
Rudi I'm so drunk.
Maria (*off*) Well, who wouldn't be?
Rudi But I like it! Maria!
Maria (*off*) Yes?
Rudi What are you doing in there?
Maria (*off*) Getting comfortable.
Rudi I wish I was.
Maria (*off*) I'll bring you a dressing-gown.
Rudi That sounds good—this jacket I borrowed is tight and uncomfortable.
Maria (*off*) Well, take it off.

Rudi takes off his jacket

Maria enters carrying a dressing-gown over her arm

Put this on and relax.

Rudi (*putting on the dressing-gown*) It's a man's dressing-gown—why do you wear a man's dressing-gown?

Maria They're better cut . . . it amuses me.

Rudi I must get one like this.

Maria Why not—and silk shirts and ties—you're going to be very rich.

Rudi Am I? I'm so drunk.

Maria Well, if you can't be drunk after tonight, when can you be?

Rudi But I was drunk all the way through the performance!

Maria Rudi!

Rudi Not with wine—with excitement and power—having that big orchestra down there do anything I want. By the way, you missed two bars in the Finale.

Maria I did nothing of the sort!

Rudi Yes, you did—and do you know why? Instead of looking at my baton, you were looking at me and that's—unprofessional.

Maria Unprofessional! I like that.

Rudi Well, it was. I could see you up on that stage looking down at me—I found that, I created it. Clever Maria!

Maria Yes, clever Maria!

Rudi Well, I'm going to tell you something, clever Maria, because I'm drunk and my tongue is very loose—you know how grateful I am to you—hearing my music played and sung like that for the first time. But you must not take me for granted, exploit me at your will.

Maria Surely you know I would never do that.

Rudi Maria. Are you in love with me?

Maria In love?

Rudi Yes. Something very exciting has happened and I don't know whether I can explain it. You and my music have become one, and as I love and respect my music, I must love and respect you.

Maria But that's what I want. (*She sings*)

No. 13   **(s) I Can Give You The Starlight**

When I was young
My foolish fancies used to make
A great mistake,
But now a little love, a little living
Has changed my ways, and taught me
And brought me
The joy of giving.
I can give you the starlight,
Love unchanging and true.
I can give you the ocean,
Deep and tender devotion.
I can give you the mountains,

       Pools of shimmering blue.
       Call and I shall be
       All you ask of me,
       Music in spring,
       Flowers for a king,
       All these I bring to you.

Rudi I wish this moment of pure happiness could last for ever.

Maria It will.

Rudi Maria, something has been worrying me.

Maria Charles?

Rudi Yes, I'd like to know.

Maria There is nothing to know.

Rudi Are you sure?

Maria Yes, it was all over long before I met you.

Rudi But people still talk . . .

Maria That's because we're friends.

Rudi I would like Charles for a friend. I would hate him to be hurt because of me.

Maria He won't be—I'm sure it's over for him as much as it is for me.

Rudi Well, then it's perfect. (*He kisses her*)

Charles suddenly enters. He carries an overnight bag

Maria (*startled*) Charles!

Charles I'm sorry to surprise you, but I'm off at dawn and I suddenly realized there were things here I would need. Hullo, Rudi, how do you feel after your great triumph? What are you doing in my dressing-gown? May I have it please, I shall want it on the train.

Rudi Your dressing-gown? I'm sorry—I didn't know it was yours.

Charles Whose else could it be?

Maria Charles, you are doing this deliberately.

Rudi takes off the dressing-gown and puts it on settee and then puts on his own jacket

Charles I should have taken it last night.

Rudi You were here last night?

Charles But of course.

Maria Tell him why you were here last night—to say goodbye.

Charles Yes, but only for a few weeks, I hope. Unless I find London a lot more exciting than I think it is. Well, Rudi, you must be delighted with your success tonight. *Lorelei* will play the whole season. Congratulations.

Rudi Thank you, Charles. I won't be using your studio again. It was very kind of you to let me have it for so long.

Charles Have I offended you in any way?

Rudi No, not at all.

Rudi moves slightly apart from Maria and Charles. He can easily overhear the next exchange between them

Maria Why are you doing this?

Charles (*snapping*) Isn't it better to hurt him a little now, than to break his heart later?

Maria Why would I ever break his heart?

Charles Because no-one has ever lasted with you.

Maria No. Until now, no-one has ever meant anything. Have I ever pretended? And just when I've found ... oh, go away ... can't you see ... this is real.

Charles exits, leaving the dressing-gown behind

Rudi moves to the window. Maria hesitates for a moment, then joins Rudi. There is silence between them for moment then Maria speaks quietly. Meanwhile, music starts under this very softly

No. 13   **(t) I Can Give You The Starlight**

Maria Rudi. Do you think I'm a liar and a cheat?

Rudi No. If you are, you must know that yourself. You said to Charles just now that this is real.

Maria And how do you know that wasn't a lie too?

Rudi I trust you.

Maria Charles came here last night to ask me to marry him or to say goodbye—we said goodbye. Do you believe me?

Rudi Yes, I believe you.

Maria And you won't think ...?

Rudi No. The past is unimportant.

They embrace in a long kiss. The music swells to a climax as——

the CURTAIN *falls*

ACT II

Scene 1

The Garden of a schloss outside Vienna. 1914. A day in late spring

When the CURTAIN *rises, Rudi is working at his piano in his summerhouse/ studio. The garden is full of Dancers and Singers. Cacille Kurt and a group of Singers are rehearsing*

(aa) When It's Spring In Vienna Page 153 I

Kurt
The winter's over
The snow is gone,
Her cloak of clover
The field puts on.
The hedgerows blossom,
All nature sings to life anew.
A song of love with a clarion ring
And lovers listen to the call of spring.
When it's spring in Vienna
The time for true lovers is near.
When the May trees bright and clear
Seem to whisper "love is near".

Chorus
When it's spring in Vienna
Our hearts are turning to love.
No more delaying,
Waltzes swaying
Bringing rapture from above.
Music compelling,
Gaily telling us
Spring is the time for love.

This number can be lengthened at will by the use of the soloist and Chorus and perhaps some Dancers. At the end of the number Rudi goes to Kurt and the Singers

Rudi That is sounding wonderful. The audience at the Gala will love it. Thank you, Cacille dear, for agreeing to take part. We are all very honoured and grateful.

Murmurs of approval from the Singers

I'll see you all at the Gala.

Kurt and the Singers exit

Rudi goes back to his piano and work

Hattie enters with a drink for Rudi

Thank you, Hattie. Oh, Hattie, never try to arrange a Gala—it's hell.
Hattie This place is bedlam. Nothing but singers and dancers.
Rudi By the way, have you seen Franzel?
Hattie He's gone to fetch Grete.
Rudi Oh yes, of course. I'd forgotten. I can hardly believe it—our Grete coming home today. Tell me, Hattie, can she really dance well? It's the new waltz, you see. They'll expect a lot—can she do it?
Hattie Of course she can. She's been a great success in England.
Rudi Our young Grete. All that in three years.
Hattie A great deal has happened in three years.
Rudi Yes. My music played and sung all over the world—and it all started in the garden—Maria—that lark's voice at six in the morning. This is all her, you know.
Hattie Why don't you two get married?
Rudi What?
Hattie You heard what I said—you haven't asked her, have you?
Rudi No.
Hattie Why ever not? She'd like it.
Rudi Hattie, I've never told this to anyone before—because I'm superstitious. I made a vow.
Hattie A vow! Who to?
Rudi To a child, to stop her heart from breaking.

Maria enters

Hullo. Where have you been?
Maria Out on the lake, studying. Hattie, bring me some iced tea, please.
Hattie Not until you've cooled down a bit. I'll bring it later on.

Hattie exits

Maria Have you been asleep?
Rudi No, just relaxing.
Maria You're happy today, aren't you? Grete's coming home. You've been good to that child. How old is she now—fifteen, sixteen?
Rudi No, she's older than that.
Maria We must look around for a nice husband for her.
Rudi A husband? For Grete? I don't think that's a very good idea.
Maria Well, I do. After all, there must be some young sprigs of nobility growing up. Oh, I forgot, I don't meet the nobility now—I'm not allowed to. They consider my position a little dubious which, of course, it is. I can sing for charity and they applaud heartily, but when you are invited to tea, I am not. It's curious, isn't it?
Rudi Do you want to go to tea?
Maria No.
Rudi Then why are you making such a fuss?
Maria Can you imagine me—sitting bolt upright and eating fancy cakes! And to think I might have been one of them.

Rudi Yes—a princess! By the way, do you ever hear from him?
Maria Who?
Rudi Charles Metterling.
Maria Funnily enough, I heard from him this morning. He's at Waldsee now—he might be coming over.
Rudi Oh, might he? That's very interesting. Yes, he might be coming over—when I invite him!
Maria When I invite him! I do believe you're jealous!
Rudi Of course I'm jealous.
Maria I worship you! I adore you! Jealous still?
Rudi Yes. And I'll still be jealous when we're very, very old with thousands of grandchildren crawling all over us.
Maria That's far too old.
Rudi All right then. Not grand—just children.
Maria Aren't you anticipating rather?
Rudi What?
Maria Children?
Rudi Well, not real ones. Just imaginary ones.
Maria You have a charming way of saying the most hurtful things.
Rudi Hurtful? I'm sorry.
Maria All right. And now shall we do some work? I don't know the last page of that song. Have you got it there?
Rudi No, but I have something else I'd like to try.
Maria What is it?
Rudi I wrote it last night.
Maria A new waltz?
Rudi No, it's not a waltz. It's a simple little tune. See if you like it.
Maria It's dedicated to me.
Rudi They're all dedicated to you—this one is specially dedicated to you.
Maria Rudi, your writing is terrible! I can't read it. You read it for me—I don't want to spoil it.

As Rudi reads Maria hums the music with each line

Rudi   "My dearest dear,
                            If I could say to you
                            In words as clear
                            As when I play to you,
                            You'd understand
                            How slight the shadow that is holding us apart.
                            So take my hand,
                            I'll lead the way for you.
                            A little waiting and you'll reach my heart."

Maria Play it for me.

Rudi plays the number and Maria sings

No. 15   **(bb) My Dearest Dear**

My dearest dear,
If I could say to you
In words as clear
As when I play to you,
You'd understand
How slight the shadow that is holding us apart.
So take my hand,
I'll lead the way for you.
A little waiting and you'll reach my heart.

Verse
Your lonely hours will spread their wings and fly;
The passing show'rs will only pass you by.
If you trust me, trust the secret in my song.
When love is true the road is never long.

My dearest dear,
If I could say to you
In words as clear
As when I play to you,
You'd understand
How slight the shadow that is holding us apart.
So take my hand,
I'll lead the way for you;
A little waiting and you'll reach my heart.

(*NB The four lines of the Verse will be found on page 22 of the* Ivor Novello Song Album, *available from Samuel French Ltd*)

(*Speaking*) Oh Rudi, I'll try not to question again. There is something I don't understand—perhaps we're not meant to. I'm content, just as we are. Are you?
Rudi Content? Don't you realize by now you're the other half of me?

They are in an embrace as:

Grete enters

Grete Hullo!
Rudi We were just——
Grete I'm sorry—I shouldn't have come this way at all.
Rudi (*pointing towards the house*) If you go over there you will——
Grete Rudi!
Rudi It's Grete! Maria, it's darling Grete!

Maria gives a reluctant sign of recognition

Grete You're Maria Zeigler, aren't you? I remember you.
Maria And you're the young girl who crawled from under the piano.
Rudi Well, I can't think what to say. I'm so ashamed I didn't recognize you.

Grete You didn't.
Rudi You've grown quite lovely! Hasn't she, Maria?
Maria Yes.
Grete I expect it's the clothes. I'm still the same.
Maria Rudi, how thoughtless we are. (*To Grete*) After your journey, you must be longing for a bath.
Grete Thank you, in a moment. I can't wait to see Hattie.
Rudi Yes, of course. Hattie! Hattie! (*He goes, shouting*) Who do you think's arrived?

Rudi exits

Grete Hattie has been so kind to me. She's written every week.
Maria I hope Rudi has too?
Grete Sometimes, but then, he's so busy.
Maria I can't tell you how excited he's been about your coming. He's talked of nothing else.

Hattie and Rudi enter

Hattie Where is she? Where is she?
Grete Hattie!

Grete and Hattie embrace

Hattie Let's look at you. So grown up! Isn't she lovely?
Maria Hattie, take her to her room—she must be exhausted.
Hattie Not yet. I want to see her here in the sunlight.
Grete Oh Hattie!

They embrace again

Hattie Did you have a good journey?

A porter and Hans, a youth, are seen carrying Grete's trunk to the house

Maria I'll see her things are put in her room.
Rudi Thank you, Maria. (*To Grete*) We've been so excited about your coming.
Maria Rudi, don't forget the rehearsal.

Maria exits

Rudi I won't.
Hattie I'll go and see about the rest of her luggage.

Hattie exits

Rudi Oh Grete.
Grete Rudi.
Rudi I was trying to think why I didn't recognize you. And now I know, it's the hair! It goes up instead of down.
Grete Thank you for sending Franzel to meet me.
Rudi He's a good friend. Did you remember him?
Grete Yes.

Rudi I'd have come myself, but . . .

Grete I know, the Gala.

Rudi I've written a new waltz which you are going to dance.

Grete Is it a lovely tune?

Rudi I think so, but then again, I would.

Grete I can't wait to hear it.

Rudi So you shall, just as soon as you've seen your room.

Franzel enters. Hattie follows

Franzel There you are! Where did you get to? By the time I'd got the luggage out of the car, you'd completely disappeared.

Grete I wanted to get in quickly.

Hattie Come along, dear—up to your room and take off those dusty clothes.

Hattie exits

Grete starts to go

Franzel Now, don't you stay away too long. Just because we've arrived, I'm not going to be ignored. How long?

Grete Twenty minutes.

Franzel Eternity!

Grete Ten minutes.

Franzel Still too long!

Grete All right, then, five.

Franzel I'll be waiting.

Grete exits

(*To Rudi*) You shouldn't do these things to me. I go to meet some schoolgirl from England, and out of the train pops that!

Rudi She's lovely, isn't she?

Franzel Yes.

Rudi Tell me, Franzel, did she talk about me?

Franzel Never stopped. "Do you think Rudi would—did you know that Rudi had—have you heard that Rudi will . . ."

Rudi She was always like that. Franzel, have you ever seen a completely happy man—because you're looking at one right now.

Franzel You haven't fallen in love with her, too, have you?

Rudi In love—with Grete? No. I love my little Grete, always have and always will. But how can I be in love twice?

Franzel Thank goodness for that! Did you notice the way she moves? I bet she's a marvellous dancer.

Rudi Yes.

Maria enters

Maria I'm sorry to interrupt this rhapsody, but Grete's having trouble with her trunk. It's stuck!

Franzel Then I'll open it. I'm an expert with trunks! Which is her room?

Maria Second on the left, first landing.
Franzel Thanks. Rudi, you won't be wanting me for a minute, will you?
Rudi No. Go on.
Franzel Good! That trunk may take a long time to open. (*To Maria*) Maria, have you ever been in love?

Franzel exits

Maria Am I right in thinking there's romance in the air?
Rudi Romance? What those two youngsters? Nonsense.
Maria Well, I don't think it's nonsense. How old is Franzel?
Rudi Twenty-four, twenty-five.
Maria That's perfect.
Rudi Why are you so anxious to marry Grete off so soon?
Maria I'm not, but I don't want her position to be dubious too. After all, what is she to you—your ward?
Rudi Not exactly—but I feel responsible for her—she has no-one else.
Maria That won't be for long. She's lovely—a nice marriage—or were you thinking of planning a career for her?
Rudi I might do worse.
Maria I'm told she dances charmingly. Why don't you write an operetta where the heroine doesn't sing a note. It happens often in England.
Rudi Perhaps she sings charmingly too.
Maria Well, she doesn't.
Rudi How do you know?
Maria First thing I asked!

Rudi roars with laughter

Why are you laughing?
Rudi I'm laughing at you! You have everything in the world and yet you're so insecure.
Maria Yes, and you've made me insecure. I don't like things and people that were in your life before me—they make me feel shut out—and when I feel shut out I do unaccountable things!
Rudi Well, don't do them here because I'm being driven mad by this Gala.
Maria What, with a new and attractive young star to add to your list of guests. Why not let her replace me—dance to all my music.
Rudi Maria, you're impossible!
Maria Yes, I *am* impossible—everything's impossible.
Rudi I can't stand this—I'm going.
Maria But what about the rehearsal?
Rudi (*shouting as he goes*) Damn the rehearsal—damn everything!

Rudi exits

Maria goes to the piano and picks up a sheet of manuscript paper and a pencil. She writes quickly

Maria (*folding the paper; calling*) Hans!

Hans enters

I want you to catch the first boat to Waldsee and deliver this personally to
Prince Charles Metterling.

Hans Yes, Fräulein.

Maria If you hurry you'll just catch the next boat. Go on—hurry!

Hans exits

Pause

Rudi enters

Rudi Maria.

Maria Don't speak to me.

Rudi Maria, I'm sorry.

Maria That's quite all right.

Rudi (*mimicking*) That's quite all right! Come on, Maria, relax.

Maria I'm sorry—but I'm all on edge.

Rudi The whole house is on edge—it's this Gala, but we mustn't let it affect
us.

Maria No, we mustn't. (*She suddenly remembers the message she has sent
with Hans*) Oh my God—Hans! Hans! Come back! It's too late, he's gone!

Rudi Where's he gone?

Maria To Pertisau—I thought of something you needed.

Rudi What was it?

Maria Manuscript paper.

Rudi I've plenty of manuscript paper.

Maria Yes. Rudi, don't you think it would be nice if we invited Charles
over?

Rudi Charles? Oh, Charles Metterling. He's at Waldsee now, isn't he?

Maria Yes . . .

Rudi Do you want me to ask him over?

Maria No, not really, but, well—I thought it might be sort of polite.

Rudi Yes, it might be sort of polite. Why don't you ask him?

Maria You don't mind?

Rudi No.

Maria Oh, I'm so stupid. If only I'd known, I could have sent Hans with a
note.

Rudi (*calling her bluff*) What time are you expecting him?

They both laugh outright

Grete and Franzel enter

Maria Did you manage the trunk?

Franzel With one flick of the wrist!

Grete I love my room!

Maria Franzel, these two haven't seen each other for three years. They have
a lot to talk about.

Franzel Yes, of course.

Maria You and I will take a walk. Rudi, what are you rehearsing first?

She pauses, seeing that he is staring at Grete

Rudi . . .

Rudi I can't remember. Oh yes, some singers and dancers from the village
are arriving at any moment. They want to show me what they are doing
for the Gala.

Maria Then we will come back in half an hour. Come along, Franzel.

Rudi Yes, that will be fine.

Maria and Franzel exit

Now I can have a good look!

Grete Will I do?

Rudi Admirably. I don't know why, I still expected bare feet and pigtails.

Grete Then you should have kept me with you.

Rudi Weren't you happy at school?

Grete Reasonably—not at first. My shoes pinched me—the girls did too.

Rudi Little beasts!

Grete I pinched them back—only harder so they stopped. I had my
calendar and I used to tear off the days one by one—but that was too
slow, so I saved up and tore off a whole month at once—it helped the time
to go more quickly. (*Pause*) Well, do you like being famous?

Rudi Yes.

Grete I saw *Lorelei* five times and *Princess in Paris* three times.

Rudi And what about the best of them all—*Love Song*?

Grete No. I read about it and it sounded much too sad and sentimental. I
don't like that sort of thing.

Rudi Oh really? So you've had no romances—no affairs of the heart?

Grete Of the heart? No. Slight holding hands at end of term dances, but
nothing to do with the heart—my heart was somewhere quite different.

Rudi Grete, you remember that last morning here before I went to Vienna,
you made me promise you something.

Grete Of course I do.

Rudi Well, I want you to know that all this time I've taken my promise to
you quite seriously ...

Grete You have?

Rudi And you know——

Hattie enters in a hurry

Hattie Rudi—the singers and the dancers are coming.

Rudi Yes, I was forgetting everything.

Hattie Here they come.

The Singers and Dancers enter. Other onlookers follow

SCENE 2

The same. Day

No. 16   **(cc) Chorale and Tyrolean Dance**

The Chorus sing unaccompanied

Chorus   Hail to the light unfading rose of dawn,
             Hail to the ray that brings this newborn day.
             Bright on the hills awaking man and beast,
             Raise the rousing anthem to the land of the East.

The orchestra joins in

             We dance till the echoes of gladness resound,
             Our rhythm goes thund'ring around and around;
             Our song of men
             For the flying and the dying of depression and tears.
             So join in our chorus and serenade the hour,
             Dispel ev'ry shadow and waken ev'ry flower,
             No voice must be silently lingering apart,
             So come, singing gaily, bringing all the joy in your heart.

The Dancers now perform their Tyrolean dance. It should be as active as possible in the choreography. At the end of the dance section the Chorus sing

             So join in our chorus and serenade the hour,
             Dispel ev'ry shadow and waken ev'ry flower,
             No voice must be silently lingering apart,
             So come, singing gaily, bringing all the joy in your heart.

The Dancers exit to the music and the Chorus follow. Rudi exits, talking to the leader of the singers. Hattie, Grete, and other onlookers exit

The Lights crossfade to give a moonlight effect on a small section of the stage as far downstage as possible. There is a bench set to one side

(dd) Music

Music plays softly as though it is coming from inside the schloss. The musical director can choose any number from the score but make it a small combination, probably a string quintet, to give the impression of music being played during dinner. The music continues into the next scene and finishes at the director's discretion

   Maria enters, followed by Charles

SCENE 3

A corner of the schloss garden. Night

Charles Maria, are you all right?
Maria Yes, thank you. It was so hot in there. I'm really quite all right.

Charles Sit down and talk to me. You know, there was no need to cut me right out of your life. It's been a success, hasn't it?

Maria Yes, of course. We're professional artists and we love each other. I'm cruel to him sometimes—particularly lately. Charles, I don't like other interests in his life. Grete—she's a sweet child and she has character, but——

Charles Yes, she's a sweet child and she has character. In fact, you're good, ordinary plain jealous.

Maria Yes, I am. I admit it. It's absurd, isn't it? Charles, why doesn't he ask me to marry him? He never has, you know. Why are you smiling?

Charles It's such a funny situation. Here am I, longing to ask you the one thing he won't.

Maria Is it because he's not sure of himself—or is he too sure of me, or have I been fooling myself all these years.

Charles Have you ever spoken to him about it?

Maria Yes, but he avoids the subject.

Charles Suppose you suddenly found out you had to get married?

Maria You mean if I were going to have a child?

Charles Yes—and you are, Maria, aren't you?

Maria Yes, I am. But why should having a child make any difference? In fact, it completes the perfect Bohemian picture. Oh Charles, I'm so unhappy.

Charles Maria, you must tell him.

Maria No. I'm sorry to have blurted it all out like this—to you of all people.

Charles Why me of all people? Why shouldn't I be the one person you should tell. After all, I've shared your happiness before, and I'd share it again.

Maria Even now?

Charles Yes.

Maria Don't say it, Charles. I might take you seriously. I don't want people to see me with my face like this. I'll walk with you to the landing stage.

Charles Yes, but you'll send me a message? I can't bear to see you unhappy. You'll let me know, either way?

Maria Either way. It's nice to know you're wanted—for certain.

Maria and Charles exit

The Lights change, taking in the main stage. The bench is left as it can be moved or used later on in next scene

SCENE 4

The garden of the schloss. A little later that night

Rudi's summer house is moved to different place for this scene

Grete and Franzel enter. Some other guests wander on

Franzel Let me come with you.

Grete No. I have to go and get the music. I won't be long. (*She begins to go*)

Franzel (*stopping her*) Grete, stay there a minute.
Grete Why?
Franzel You look so lovely.
Grete Do I? Franzel, you say the nicest things, just when they're wanted. I could almost kiss you.
Franzel "Almost"?

Grete kisses him and then exits. Rudi enters

Rudi I know—you've been kissed.
Franzel Yes.
Rudi When you've recovered, perhaps you could organize some chairs.
Franzel Yes.

Franzel exits

Rudi goes to the piano

Hattie, Lotte and the Guests enter—some with chairs

Lotte Well, where's the entertainment? Who's doing what?

Franzel enters with chairs

Franzel Grete's getting the music. She's singing for us.

The remainder of the Guests and Grete enter

Lotte (*taking charge*) Come on everybody, quickly find yourselves a seat. Grete's going to sing. (*To Rudi*) What's it going to be—a turkey trot?
Rudi Nothing so modern. It's just one of those little musical comedy numbers that are so popular in England and nowhere else.
Lotte Sounds delightful. (*She sits with Franzel*)
Grete Here it is, Rudi.
Rudi What's it called?
Grete "Primrose". I don't sing like Maria, you know that.
Rudi Never mind. What exactly are you going to do?
Grete A verse and a chorus. Then a dance. Shall we start, Rudi?
Rudi You must tell me if it's the correct time, because I'm not used to these new rhythms. (*He plays the introduction*) Is that all right?

No. 18

Grete nods then she sings and dances the "Primrose" number accompanied by Rudi on the piano

(ee) Primrose

Grete   Every other Sunday afternoon
                             Walking till the summer Sunday moon
                             Shines above her,
                             You'll love her, Miss Primrose.
                             See her parasol beneath the trees,
                             Dainty as a flower and Japanese,
                             When she walks out with her Pekinese,
                             Miss Primrose.

Primrose was a naughty little blossom,
And she lived on Primrose Hill,
And she always dressed to kill,
When she went up West
And did her best.
Primrose used to come home rather later
Than the decent hour that pleased her mater,
Knowing her daughter
Ought'er be kept a prim Primrose.

Grete dances. At the end of the dance she repeats part of the refrain

Grete is obviously a success with the guests

   Maria enters

She takes in the scene—particularly noting the fuss being made of Grete by the guests and by Rudi

Maria I'm sorry to break up this happy gathering, but we have to make an early start for the Gala in the morning. Rudi, I think we should all go to bed.
Lotte But we're having such fun, Maria. It's too early for bed.
Rudi No, Lotte, Maria is quite right. We have to get up very early in the morning—five o'clock. Off to bed, all of you.

Lotte stays seated

   You too, Lotte. After all, you are in charge tomorrow. Good-night!

   Lotte and the Guests go, taking their chairs with them

Grete and Franzel move downstage to the bench

Maria Rudi, I want to talk to you.
Rudi What, now?
Maria Yes—alone. It's important.
Rudi Just give me about ten minutes and when you hear me play this (*he plays a few bars of "My Dearest Dear"*) you'll know I'm free and then come.   No. 18a
Maria All right.

   Maria exits

(ff) My Dearest Dear (Reprise)

Rudi continues to play "My Dearest Dear"

SCENE 5

A corner of the schloss garden. Immediately following

Franzel You know, there'll never be another moon like this.
Grete I know, and I can see it from my bedroom window.
Franzel But I won't be there.

Grete goes towards Rudi. Franzel follows

SCENE 6

The garden of the schloss. Immediately following

Grete goes to Rudi. Rudi stops playing

Grete Rudi, will you call your puppy away—he's biting my ankle again.
Rudi Franzel, go to bed, please.
Franzel Oh lord, I'm always being sent to bed.
Grete It's the right place for young boys.
Franzel I can give you ten years.
Grete I wish you would. Go on—go to bed now and I'll sit with you in the front of your car tomorrow.
Rudi Oh lord, then we'll all go over the cliff.
Franzel Good-night.
Rudi Good-night, Franzel.

Franzel exits

Rudi Well, how many times has he asked you to marry him?
Grete Six or seven—I'm afraid I haven't counted.
Rudi Oh. It sounds as if you don't care for the idea?
Grete I haven't really thought about it.
Rudi Hadn't you better?
Grete Why?
Rudi All sorts of reasons. For one, Franzel's a very nice person.
Grete I don't think that's enough.
Rudi And he's also a dear friend of mine.
Grete That's more encouraging.
Rudi And he's very much in love with you.
Grete Well, I'm not very much in love with him.
Rudi That makes it a little difficult. And you think you never could be?
Grete I think it's very difficult to get mumps when you've already got mumps.
Rudi Mumps are what children get!
Grete That doesn't make them any less painful.
Rudi Grete, I'm years older than you, and I'm not quite the same person you knew.
Grete You mean you're rich now, instead of poor, famous instead of unknown?

Rudi Yes, but that's unimportant. There are other things . . .

Grete Shall we take the other things for granted? I don't think I could bear to hear you talk of them. Poor Rudi—it's difficult for you, isn't it? It mustn't be. I understand and I'm going to be sensible. Just do one thing for me—I want you to keep your vow—the one you made to stop me crying. It's all right, you needn't worry about my answer. It's just that I want to be able to say—"He did ask me. Of course, I refused, but he did ask me".

Rudi And I thought you hadn't grown up.

Grete Perhaps I haven't. Perhaps this is my last fling of childishness.

Rudi And you really want me to do this?

Grete Yes.

Rudi What do you want me to say?

Grete What you would say, if you cared.

Rudi If I cared, in that way, I would say . . . (*He hesitates*)

Maria appears and listens

"Grete, darling Grete—you know everything about me that there is to know—I'm years older than you. I'm dreadfully selfish, incurably ambitious, a supreme egoist, in fact, altogether the last person in the world you should marry, but in spite of all that, I'm asking, will you?"

Maria hurriedly turns away and exits

Grete What was that?

Rudi I didn't hear anything. Well, I'm waiting.

Grete Poor Rudi, wouldn't it be awful for you if I said "yes".

Rudi Oh Grete, you wouldn't, would you?

Grete No, and that's the first thing you've said that makes me know you're just the same. Rudi, you won't ever laugh at me about this, will you? And you won't ever tell Maria—even when you're married. You are going to be married, aren't you?

Rudi Yes. And do you know, you're the reason we haven't been. My promise to you has always stopped me.

Grete Then I *am* important to you?

Rudi Of course you are. You were the first person who ever believed in my music.

Grete I'll always remember that and when I'm famous, people will say "Yes—and you know she turned down Rudi Kleber". You won't mind if I boast a little, will you?

Grete kisses Rudi on the cheek

Grete Good-night, dear Rudi. I hope I won't disgrace you in the Gala tomorrow.

Rudi Oh, I don't think that's likely—not after what I've seen tonight. Good-night, and God bless you for being so completely understanding.

Grete Grey hairs—I've never noticed them before.

Rudi They weren't there five minutes ago. Grete, try and be nice to Franzel—please.

Grete I shall be angelic to Franzel. I can afford to be now. Rudi, thank you for giving me the first refusal.

Grete exits

Rudi plays part of "My Dearest Dear" and looks for Maria. When she does not come, he stops playing to look for her

Rudi (*calling*) Maria!

Not finding her, he runs off

(*Calling as he goes*) Maria!

The Lights crossfade to a small section downstage which represents outside the Gala

SCENE 7

Outside the Gala. Night

Lotte and Franzel enter. Lotte is dressed in an exotic fancy dress (maybe Spanish). Franzel is in a more discreet form of fancy dress costume (basically "tails"). Lotte is checking a list of notes

Lotte (*firmly in charge*) Have all the performers arrived? (*Before Franzel can answer*) Have they all eaten? No-one's sick, or anything silly, like that?

Franzel Grete's very nervous. It's unfair to expect her to open the Gala with her dance. It's too important. You should——

Lotte Never mind what I should have done. I would never have dared to ask a local group to open. Besides, we can't give Grete special treatment—you know how people gossip and jump to the wrong conclusions. Maria's the star tonight—she's the one they all want to see.

Franzel As you say Lotte, but I still think——

Lotte Stop behaving like a lovesick juvenile. Go and see if we have enough people to start and, if there are, announce the first item. I want to check the catering.

Lotte exits

Franzel turns and walks upstage. As he does, the Lights come up on the Gala set

The Audience, in fancy dress, are all waiting. They include Cacille Kurt, Ceruti, and Rudi, who stands apart from the rest of the Audience. Footmen stand on the fringe of the Audience

SCENE 8

The Gala. Night

The Gala is held in a square which has coloured lights and suitable decorations

Franzel greets some people then indicates to an unseen orchestra. There is a drum roll or equivalent

Franzel Ladies and gentlemen. Welcome to our Gala. The first item on our programme is "The Leap Year Waltz". Rudi Kleber has written it specially for Miss Grete Schone and some members of the Corps de Ballet of the Theater an der Wien.

The Audience clap and settle

Miss Grete Schone and "The Leap Year Waltz".

Lotte enters and joins the Audience

(hh) The Leap Year Waltz   No. 21

Grete and her male dancing partner enter with the Dancing Chorus and perform the waltz

Rudi watches but also searches the crowd for Maria. The waltz finishes and the Audience applauds

Grete and the Dancers exit

Rudi and Franzel meet. Background music from the orchestra starts

(ii) Incidental Music   No. 23

Rudi (*to Franzel*) Any sign of Maria yet?
Franzel No. Where's she been all day?
Rudi I don't know.
Franzel She must be here soon. Her song comes immediately after supper.
Rudi She hasn't even rehearsed it with the orchestra.

Grete enters

Franzel Grete, you were wonderrful.
Rudi Yes, delightful.
Grete Rudi, what's the matter?
Rudi It's Maria. We don't know where she is. No-one's seen her all day. You were right. She must have overheard last night.
Grete Well, you can explain that in a moment.
Rudi If I could find her.

Maria enters

Maria (*to a Footman*) Can you tell me how I get out of this place? I want my car.
Footman Yes, madam, follow me.

The Footman goes

Maria starts to follow but Lotte sees her and goes to her

Lotte Maria, you can't leave. What about your song?
Maria (*stopping*) I'm tired. I've had a very busy day.

Rudi has also seen Maria and joins her and Lotte

Rudi So busy that you couldn't even come to rehearsal?

Maria That's what is upsetting you.

Rudi No, not that. I wanted to explain something to you.

Maria About the song?

Rudi No. Maria, I must talk to you alone.

Maria I don't think there's anything you can say to me alone that cannot be said in public.

Lotte Maria, what's upset you? You're just overtired. Shall I get you a drink or something?

Maria No thank you, Lotte. I have some marvellous news for you. Congratulations, Rudi—I wish you and Grete every happiness. That's my news. Rudi has asked Grete to marry him and she has accepted.

Lotte reacts and, for once, before she can speak

Rudi This is a terrible misunderstanding——

Maria Misunderstanding? But you did ask her to marry you?

Rudi In a way—yes ...

Maria Luckily or unluckily, I overheard you.

Rudi And if you'd waited you would have heard Grete refuse——

Grete Yes, Maria—Rudi asked me to marry him because he once gave me his word that he would—and he kept his word just to please me. Now, won't you forget all about it. It was nothing—just a childish joke.

Maria Childish joke! I don't think I'm very good at childish jokes. (*She moves as if to go*)

Rudi follows Maria. She stops. The music finishes

Rudi Maria, I assure you that's all it was. I nearly went mad last night wondering where you were—and today, no word from you. You could have trusted me. Don't look so tragic. It's all right now, isn't it?

They are now apart from the others

Maria Rudi, when I ran away from you last night, I went to where I knew I would find comfort, security and faithfulness. My whole world has crumbled about me. I've loved you so much.

Rudi But I tried to explain to you. The song I wrote—I asked you to wait. That's what it meant.

Maria Don't, Rudi, please. I married Charles Metterling this morning.

Rudi What are you saying?

Maria I married Charles Metterling this morning.

Rudi No!

Maria That's what I meant by comfort, security, faithfulness ...

Maria exits

Grete (*going to Rudi*) Rudi?

Rudi She was my whole world—my music too.

Music, slow waltz, starts. People begin to dance

(jj) Waltz   No. 24

Grete You've still got that part of her. Nothing can take that away.

Rudi What's that dirge they're playing? I didn't write that as a funeral march, I wrote it as a waltz, a happy waltz! Now, take your time from me. One, two, three, one, two, three, one, two, three!

Grete and Franzel exit during the mêlée which ensues after Rudi has spoken. Rudi hurries out through the dancers

At the end of the quick waltz there is a sudden stop. Black-out

Everyone exits

(kk) Music (Incidental Waltz)   No. 26

Immediately the orchestra should start to play scene change cover music which should have a twenties feel to it in contrast to the typical Viennese Waltz sound we have had previously. It is important that it should be a small combination of a lead trumpet and a few strings with percussion. The choice of the music from the vocal score is left to the musical director who will know the possibilities within the orchestral set-up, but it could be "Incidental Waltz", No. 26 in the vocal score

The set for Locher's restaurant comes on. This is probably two small trucks, one from each side meeting centre stage. One truck has a table and two chairs, unoccupied at the moment. The other truck has Rudi, Grete and Franzel, sitting at a table having just finished dinner. Rudi and Franzel (who could have a moustache) are in single-breasted dinner jackets with black bow-ties and wing collars, Grete is dressed in twenties style. The tables are arranged so that people are prevented from seeing those at the adjoining table. Oscar, the head waiter, is at his small, tall table on which the bookings diary is kept. If there can be a few steps near to him, coming down from off stage for Maria's entrance and exit, it would be helpful

The music should stop just before the dialogue starts

SCENE 9

Locher's restaurant. 1927. Night

Rudi is sitting at a table with Franzel and Grete

Grete You're very preoccupied.

Rudi Am I? It's this place. It gives me the shivers.

Grete Memories?

Rudi Yes. Locher's as it was, nearly thirteen years ago. Do you remember it then, Franzel? Oscar tells me my friends can't afford to come here any more.

Franzel Dear old Oscar—many's the time he's poured me into a cab at dawn. People don't know how to get drunk these days.
Grete You should see New York. Rudi, we must take him with us when we go back.
Rudi I may not be going back to New York.
Grete But Rudi, why stay in a place so full of memories?
Rudi Perhaps that's why I want to stay.
Franzel Do take me with you if you go back to America. I'm sick of trying to sell cars that won't go, to people who can't pay.
Rudi In what capacity would you go to America?
Franzel As her husband.
Grete Indeed! And what have you to offer me?
Franzel Six good suits and a beautiful nature.
Grete Any money?
Franzel Certainly not—don't be vulgar. Have you?
Grete Pots.
Franzel Thank the lord for that. If you'd said that you were poor but honest, I'd have cried off. Well, is it on?

No. 5a

(ll) Waltz Of My Heart

The orchestra starts playing "Waltz Of My Heart", again with a twenties feel and trumpet lead. Continue until the number is played through

Grete I can't say yet. I shall have to ask Rudi, see what he thinks.
Franzel Of course.
Rudi Go and dance. Go on. You know you're dying to.
Grete Are you sure you don't mind?
Rudi Why should I mind? They're playing one of my waltzes.
Grete Come on, Franzel.

Grete and Franzel rise and go off, supposedly to the dance floor

In another part of the restaurant, Oscar, the head waiter, is with Maria. He takes the cloak, or top coat, she is wearing.

Oscar Your usual place, Highness? If I had known you were coming, I would have had your favourite roses on the table.
Maria Thank you, Oscar.
Oscar Will His Excellency be joining you?
Maria No, he has an official engagement.
Oscar May I order for you?
Maria Not yet. I'll call you when I'm ready.
Oscar Then let me show you to your table.
Maria Thank you.

He takes Maria to the table next to Rudi who is being served coffee

Rudi (*to the Waiter*) Thank you.

Rudi starts to hum the refrain of "Waltz Of My Heart" and Maria takes it up where he leaves off

Maria (*singing*)   Ring out your bells for me,
                               Ivory keys,
                               Weave out your spells for me,
                               Orchestra please!

Rudi My tune, I think.

Maria No mine. It was given to me.

Rudi By whom?

Maria By someone I hoped I'd forgotten.

Rudi By someone who hoped he'd forgotten you.

Maria How wrong we were.

Rudi (*rising*) I can't get over it. My first night to Vienna after nearly thirteen years, I come into Locher's and in you walk.

Maria (*rising*) And I haven't been here for months. Strange, isn't it?

Rudi I would have known you anywhere.

Maria I wouldn't have known you. So sleek, well-dressed—confident. I'm sure that jacket isn't tight and uncomfortable.

Rudi No. And the whole suit is entirely mine, although it's not yet paid for.

Maria That's because you're rich. Only the poor pay cash. I'm right, aren't I? (*She sits at Rudi's table*)

Rudi (*sitting*) I've been lucky.

Maria And prolific. A Kleber Operetta a year. I never realized how important money is, Rudi. We have very little now.

Rudi You still have your voice.

Maria Which I seldom use.

Rudi A pity.

Maria Yes. (*Pause*) I've written to you several times.

Rudi I've never received any letters.

Maria I never posted them. The best letters are seldom posted.

Rudi Never mind. You're here now.

Maria You never married?

Rudi reacts

No. I would have heard. And what happened to Grete?

(mm) My Dearest Dear (Reprise)   No. 26a

The orchestra softly starts playing "My Dearest Dear" with a twenties feel to it. Continue until the number is played through

Rudi (*pointing off*) She's over there, dancing with Franzel. She's very successful in America. How are things with you?

Maria Oh, I lead a very interesting life. My official duties keep me busy. I don't really have much time to think . . .

Rudi Are you happy?

Maria Does that matter? That song . . .

Rudi Yes, that song.

Maria I know it by heart, even now—every word—every note . . . (*She sings softly*)

My dearest dear,
If I could say to you
In words so clear
As when I play to you,
You'd understand . . .

She breaks down

Rudi Maria, I can't bear to see you so unhappy. Come back to me—it isn't too late. Your marriage to Charles was based on a misunderstanding between you and me. If he realizes that he'll let you go. He must.

Maria But it's over twelve years ago, Rudi. You can't brush aside all those years just like that. I must go on.

Rudi Why? Look at me. Can you honestly tell me you've had one moment of happiness since we parted? You see, you can't. You've been trying to be someone else and what's the result? You're unhappy and defeated, we both are. Don't let's pretend. Maria, we can still have the future. It's for you to decide.

Maria No, Rudi. You must decide.

Rudi Then I've decided, here, tonight.

Maria Not tonight. A week from now I shall come to you, wherever you say. You can tell me then what I must do.

Rudi What difference will a week make?

Maria Perhaps nothing, perhaps everything. I must go. A week from now. (*She rises*)

Rudi Where? (*He rises*)

Maria I'll leave that to you. Send me word.

No. 13   **(nn) I Can Give You The Starlight**

The orchestra plays the number through in twenties style for the scene change (finishing the moment Rudi enters for the next scene)

Rudi I know where. Maria—stay there a moment.

Maria stops and turns

It's all right—I just wanted to be sure I hadn't seen a ghost.

Oscar gives Maria her cloak or topcoat

Maria exits

Rudi indicates that he would like his coat and hat. Oscar brings them and helps Rudi into the coat (which should be dark for evening wear with, perhaps, an astrakhan collar—this will enable it to double as a topcoat for Rudi for the next scene. The hat can be a black homburg). While Rudi is putting on his coat and hat, the scene change should start

Rudi walks off

SCENE 10

The beer garden of a schloss outside Vienna. Day

There are lights in the trees. In one corner, downstage, there is a small piano on a rostrum with maybe one or two more instruments. The place should feel different from the previous scenes, without too much obvious change

Hattie and a Waitress are tidying up

   Rudi enters

Hattie Rudi!

Rudi Hattie! Younger and prettier than ever.

Hattie Not me. A bit whiter on top now.

Rudi It suits you.

Hattie Let's have a look at you. You've changed.

Rudi Not too much, I hope?

Hattie In the right way. You've got a wise look now. Think the little place looks nice?

Rudi Yes, and you're happy here?

Hattie Happier than I've ever been in my life—and it's all thanks to you. Whatever made you buy it for me?

Rudi I wanted to be sure there was one garden in the world I could walk into and would always remain unchanged. Oh, I take it all back. What's this? Lights in the trees—and an orchestra! Hattie, this is sacrilege ...

Hattie Well, you know how it is, dear—people like that kind of thing these days. You've got to move with the time, you know.

There is the noise of a car approaching

Rudi There's a car coming up hill. It must be her.

Hattie Her?

Rudi Yes—Maria.

Hattie Maria? But she's——

Rudi I know. She's a Princess and it's all very difficult, but it will work out, you'll see. Hattie, you know I love you very much, but you must go away right now. Right away.

Hattie I can't get over it. Do you want coffee, dear?

Rudi No, I don't want any coffee. Just go away.

   Hattie goes

   Maria enters

Rudi goes to meet her

Maria I'm not late, am I?

Rudi No, I was just terrified in case you hadn't received my letter.

Maria Of course I did, and even before I'd opened it, I knew we would meet here.

Rudi Was it difficult to get away?

Maria No, not really. I simply said I was tired and needed the country air. Charles said I was looking pale.

Rudi You're looking lovely.

Maria I shouldn't be. I haven't been sleeping well all this week.

Rudi Maria, why did you say it would be for me to decide?

Maria It still is.

Rudi I don't understand. You're here . . .

Maria Yes, but I didn't come alone. I do hope you won't think I've taken an unfair advantage of you. You see, I have someone else to consider.

Rudi Someone else?

Maria goes and waves

  Carl, a boy of about twelve, comes in

Maria Now, go and say "How do you do"—nicely.

Carl How do you do, sir.

Rudi How do you do!

They shake hands

Carl I'm Carl Metterling.

Rudi Rudi Kleber.

Carl Is that short for Rudolf?

Rudi Yes, I believe it is.

Carl I'm sometimes called Carlo—but that's not short for Carl, in fact, it's longer. My mother calls me Carlo, don't you, Mama?

Maria Herr Kleber writes some of the music you've heard me sing.

Carl I should like to write music. Is it very difficult?

Rudi No, not very.

Carl Is it anything like typewriting?

Maria Charles gave him a typewriter for Christmas—he drives us mad with it.

Rudi How old are you, Carl?

Carl Nearly thirteen.

Rudi and Maria's eyes meet

Rudi I see.

Carl Mama, was it true about the coffee creme, or were you making that up?

Maria No, I wasn't. If you go in there and say you're Maria Zeigler's son, a very nice old lady will give you the best coffee creme you've ever had.

Carl Shall I see you again, sir?

Rudi I hope so.

Carl I hope so, too.

  Carl runs off to find Hattie

There is silence between Maria and Rudi. Maria sits

Maria I wanted you to see Carlo.

Rudi sits

Rudi Does Charles know?

Maria Yes, he knew from the first.

Rudi He must love you very much.

Maria He does.

Rudi And you?

Maria I'm grateful.

Rudi Is that enough? Maria, why didn't you tell me?

Maria I tried to that night.

Rudi That night . . .

Maria Rudi, are you still asking me to go away with you? It would mean a clean break?

Rudi The boy, too?

Maria Charles loves him as if he were his own son. The world, too, takes it for granted that he is. They're devoted to each other. It's a secure little world for him. I don't think we can just smash that world to pieces.

Rudi Maria, is it any comfort to know he's our son?

Maria Yes.

Rudi Talk to him for me. Play him some of my music. Then, if we ever meet, we won't be complete strangers.

Maria I promise.

Rudi Maria, there's not much time and I have so many things to say. I love you and only you. You have always been the colour and the magic in my life and nothing can ever take that away. There is so much unrest and unhappiness in the world. We are going to see great changes. We will almost forget to smile and make music, but not quite. I know, I feel it. One day, we'll wake as if from an evil dream and forget to hate, and the world will smile again and music and friendship will once more be important. Keep me in your heart as I will keep you in mine. I won't even be unhappy now I know we have something to share.

Carl enters carrying a cake box

Carl Mama?

Maria I'm here, Carl.

Carl Look, Mama, she gave me all these lovely cakes. Can I take them back to school? She said it would be all right.

Maria Did you thank her properly?

Carl Yes—I actually kissed her, but she didn't mind. Will you be coming back to Vienna with us, sir?

Rudi No, I'm afraid not.

Carl I'm sorry.

Rudi Yes, I'm sorry too, Carlo. Forgive me. I should have said Carl.

Carl No, please, Carlo—it's much more friendly.

Rudi Yes, it's much more friendly.

Maria Now, say goodbye to Herr Kleber and wait for me in the car.

Carl Goodbye, sir.

Rudi Goodbye, Carlo. I will always remember our meeting.

Carl exits

Maria I hope I did right in bringing him?

Rudi Yes.

Maria We won't say goodbye, will we? I don't think I could. But do something for me. Go and sit at the piano, where I first saw you, long before you saw me, and play for me.

No. 26a   **(oo) My Dearest Dear** (Reprise)

Rudi goes slowly to the piano and starts to play "My Dearest Dear" very softly. Maria hums and then as she starts to exit she sings it very tenderly

Maria   You'd understand
                         How slight the shadow that is holding us apart.
                         So take my hand
                         I'll lead the way for you
                         A little waiting and you'll reach my heart.

The Lights fade to a spot on Rudi as Maria finishes the song and the scene begins to be struck

Maria exits

Rudi sits weeping, then closes the piano lid

Rudi slowly exits. The "orchestra", on its rostrum, is pulled off

No. 28   **(pp) Finale**

A spot comes up on Grete upstage centre

The Finale and Curtain Call sequence begins as Grete dances forward, until she reaches halfway

Rudi and Maria join Grete, then the rest of the company join

The Finale should finish on "Waltz Of My Heart" sung by Maria with all the Chorus joining in. Then into choreographed curtain calls, finishing with a reprise of "Waltz Of My Heart" with everyone singing

CURTAIN

Playout music

LIGHTING PLOT

Practical fittings required: coloured lights in trees for Act II Scene 8

Various interior and exterior settings

ACT I

To open: Black-out

Cue 1	When ready *Bring up dim lighting upstage*	(Page 1)
Cue 2	As sound effects stop *Snap on harsh white spot on* **Goetzer** R *and harsh white follow spot on* **Rudi** L	(Page 1)
Cue 3	**Goetzer:** "... you won't be released." *Snap off spot on* **Goetzer** R, *fade out upstage lighting*	(Page 1)
Cue 4	As **Maria Zeigler** enters L *Bring up follow spot on* **Maria**, *adding warmth to both spots*	(Page 2)
Cue 5	**Maria** and **Rudi** turn to look upstage *Bring up follow spot on* **Grete** *upstage* C	(Page 2)
Cue 6	**Rudi** and **Maria** exit *Snap off spots on* **Rudi** *and* **Maria**	(Page 2)
Cue 7	When Scene 2 is set *Bring up overall exterior dawn effect*	(Page 2)
Cue 8	**Rudi** and **Grete** exit *Quick fade to Black-out, then bring up strobe effect for music (e)*	(Page 4)
Cue 9	When men and women have arrived *Cut strobe and bring up light morning sunshine effect*	(Page 5)
Cue 10	As **Maria** finishes singing *Fade to spots on* **Maria** *and* **Rudi**	(Page 9)
Cue 11	When solo violin finishes *Black-out. When ready bring up full general lighting*	(Page 9)
Cue 12	After **Chorus** exits *Crossfade to daylight effect downstage*	(Page 10)
Cue 13	**Grete** follows **Rudi** to wave goodbye *Fade to follow spot on* **Grete**	(Page 12)

Cue 14	**Grete** exits	(Page 12)
	Crossfade to full interior day effect	
Cue 15	At the end of "Wings Of Sleep"	(Page 15)
	Fade to Black-out, then bring up working lights	
Cue 16	As **Ceruti** sings "My Life Belongs To You"	(Page 16)
	Crossfade to 2 spots giving exterior moonlight effect on **Maria** *and* **Ceruti**	
Cue 17	At the end of "My Life Belongs To You"	(Page 17)
	Black-out	
Cue 18	To open Scene 7	(Page 17)
	Bring up interior effect downstage	
Cue 19	To open Scene 8	(Page 19)
	Crossfade to "theatrical" effect	
Cue 20	At the end of "Lady Enchanting" Reprise	(Page 20)
	Black-out	
Cue 21	To open Scene 9	(Page 21)
	Bring up interior effect downstage	
Cue 22	As corridor piece is flown out	(Page 21)
	Crossfade to overall interior effect with night effect outside window	

ACT II

To open: Bright exterior daylight effect

Cue 23	**Hattie, Grete** and the other **onlookers** exit	(Page 34)
	Crossfade to moonlight effect downstage	
Cue 24	**Maria** and **Charles** exit	(Page 35)
	Crossfade to overall night light with garden lights effect	
Cue 25	**Rudi** exits	(Page 40)
	Crossfade to moonlight effect downstage	
Cue 26	**Franzel** turns and walks upstage	(Page 40)
	Bring up general night effect with practicals on	
Cue 27	As music No. 24 stops	(Page 43)
	Black-out	
Cue 28	To open Scene 9	(Page 43)
	Bring up overall interior effect	
Cue 29	**Rudi** walks off	(Page 46)
	Brings up overall daylight effect	
Cue 30	As **Maria** finishes singing	(Page 50)
	Fade to spot on **Rudi**	

Cue 31   **Rudi** exits   (Page 50)
           Crossfade to follow spot on **Grete** *upstage*

Cue 32   As **Rudi, Maria** and the **Company** enter   (Page 50)
           Increase to full general lighting

EFFECTS PLOT

ACT I

Cue 1   As the CURTAIN rises   (Page 1)
Sound track of a goose-stepping march*, gradually increase to climax, then cut

Cue 2   **Maria:** "... I would even give up the stage——"   (Page 13)
Door bangs shut

ACT II

Cue 3   **Hattie:** "... move with the time, you know."   (Page 47)
Sound of car approaching and eventually pulling up

MADE AND PRINTED IN GREAT BRITAIN BY
LATIMER TREND & COMPANY LTD PLYMOUTH
MADE IN ENGLAND